Everyday Maths

Out and about

Annie Owen

WAYLAND

Everyday Maths

At Home
Fun with Food
Ourselves
Out and About

First published in 1995 by Wayland (Publishers) Ltd,
61 Western Avenue, Hove, East Sussex BN3 1JD

© Copyright 1995 Wayland (Publishers) Ltd

British Library Cataloguing in Publication Data

Owen, Annie
Out and About. – (Everyday Maths)
I. Title II. Series
510

ISBN 0-7502-1395-7

Printed and bound in Italy by Rotolito Lombarda, S.p.A., Milan
Design and typesetting by Can Do Design, Buckingham
Illustrations by Clare Mattey

Picture acknowledgements
APM Studios Cover; Brian Armson 5, 12, 13; Greg Evans International 1, 8, 14, 26; Sally and Richard Greenhill 4, 18, 20 (both), 22, 23; Tony Stone Images 6, 10; Wayland 24.

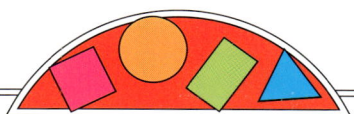

Contents

A walk in the woods	4
Going to school	6
At the park	8
A train journey	10
Shopping for food	12
The funfair	14
Rollercoaster game	16
On the lake	18
At the zoo	20
Going for a swim	22
A plane journey	24
At the seaside	26
Glossary	28
Notes for parents and teachers	30
Index	32

Words in **bold** in the text are explained in the Glossary on page 28.

 This symbol shows there is an activity to be completed.

A walk in the woods

This family is going to have a picnic in the park. The children are going to look for different flowers and insects.

Insects always have six legs. Spiders always have eight legs. Which of these are insects? Write down their names.

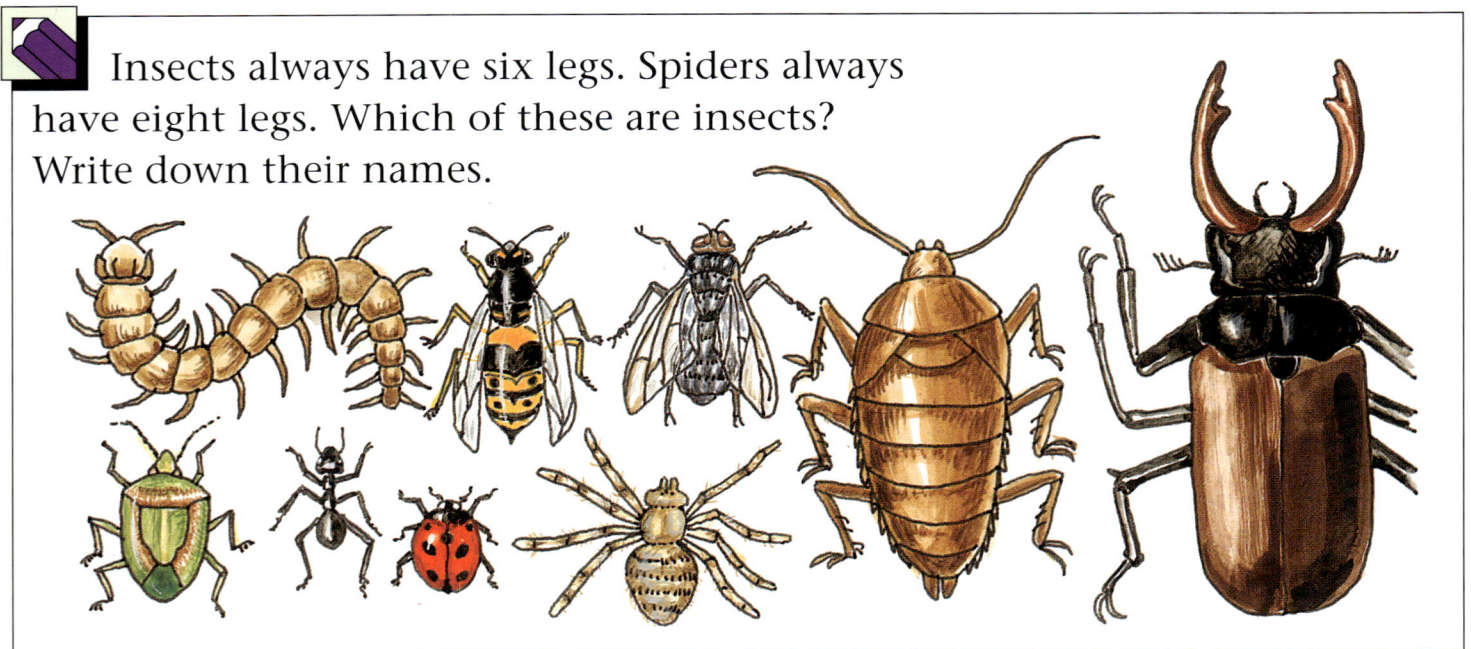

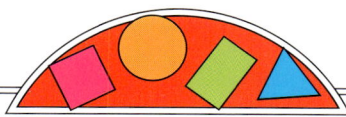

Butterflies are insects. Their wings are **symmetrical**. This means that one side looks like a mirror picture of the other side.

Copy these butterflies on to some paper. Draw in the patterns on the missing sides. The first one is done for you.

Some flowers are symmetrical too. Draw some flowers with 2, 3, 4, 5, and 6 petals. Which ones are symmetrical?

Going to school

Many children live close to school. They walk to school each day.

Come out of the house.

Turn right.

Walk to the cross-roads.

Turn left. Walk to the cross-roads.

Turn right. Take the next left.

Turn right into school.

Here are the **directions** to get from Frank's house to school. Follow them on the map on page 7 and see if they are right.

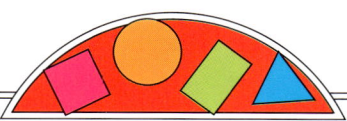

Can you find the **route** from Saira's house to the school? Follow the route with your finger on the map. Write down the directions on a piece of paper.

Guess the answers to these questions. Does Frank or Saira live closer to the school? Who lives closer to the park?

Use a piece of string to check your answers.

At the park

When Zoë goes to the park she likes to climb in the adventure playground.

Here are some shapes and their names. How many of these shapes do you know? Look around. Can you see any of these shapes? Test your friends, to see how many shapes they can name.

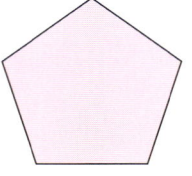 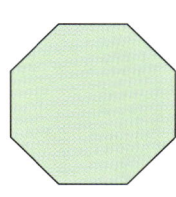 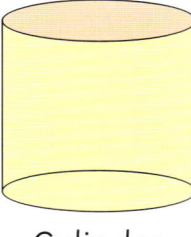 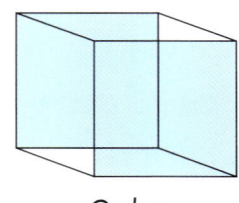 

Pentagon   Octagon   Cylinder   Cube   Square

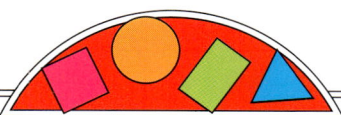

How many shapes can you find in this picture? How many **pentagons** can you see? Are there any **octagons**? What other shapes can you see and name?

Make a list and record your answers like this.

square	///
rectangle	𝍫𝍫 //
cube	
triangle	
pentagon	
octagon	

A train journey

Tom and Jenny are going to visit their grandmother in Newsea. They are going on a train with their aunt. They look at the timetable to find out when the trains go to Newsea.

Trains to Newsea	
Platform 3	9.30
	11.00
	12.30
	14.00
	15.30
	17.00
	18.30

 How often do the trains go to Newsea?

The train journey takes two and a half hours. If Tom and Jenny catch the 11 o'clock train, what time will they arrive at Newsea? If they catch the next train, what time will they arrive?

Each carriage on the toytown train has seats for 4 people. At least two people must sit in each carriage. This train has 17 people on it. The people are sitting in the carriages like this:
4 + 2 + 3 + 4 + 2 + 2

Can you think of other ways for 17 people to sit on the train? How would you seat 16 people in the carriages? Draw a train and the people in the carriages to show how you would do this.

Shopping for food

Freddie's family buy bread at the baker's shop. Sometimes they buy cakes as well. Freddie likes the buns with cherries best.

Today the baker has a bag of 30 cherries for the buns. He could put 1 cherry on top of each bun and make 30 buns. If he puts 2 cherries on top of each bun, how many buns could he make? Draw your buns like this to help you.

What happens if he puts 3 cherries on each bun?

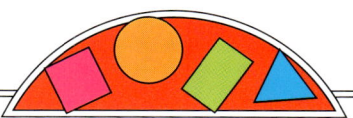

Gregory goes to the supermarket with his mum or dad once a week. Before they go, they make a list of the things they want to buy.

▼ Here is the list.

Milk

Jam

Bread

Butter

Potatoes

Rice

Spaghetti

Tomatoes

Cheese

Help Gregory to find all the food on the list. Try to find the shortest route round the supermarket for Gregory. Use string to help you.

Way Out ↓   Way In ↑

The funfair

How many horses can you see on this merry-go-round?

Here is a picture of a merry-go-round from the air. Can you see the pattern?

Draw the pattern on paper. Colour the inside circle of horses in red. Colour the next circle of horses in blue. Choose a different colour for each of the other circles and colour them.

Write out the number pattern like this.

There are . . . . . red horses

There are . . . . . blue horses

There are . . . . .

What happens to the numbers in the pattern?

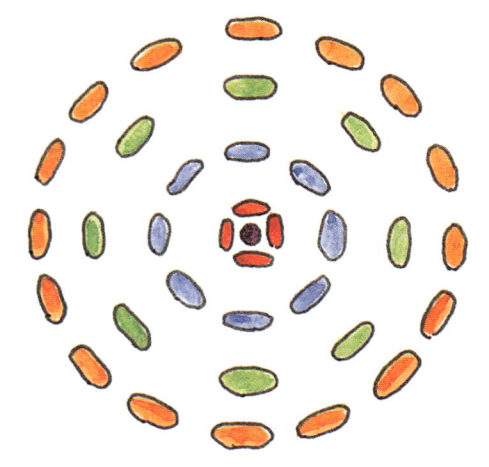

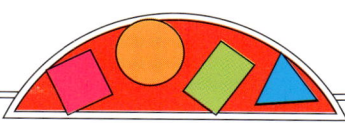

The children are fishing for plastic fish. The fish are numbered 1, 2, 3, 4, 5, or 6. If they get a fish with a 6 on it they will win a prize. Do they have a good chance of winning?

If Lara has 3 turns at fishing will she win a prize? If she has 6 turns will she win?

Lucky Fish
10p a go

Find out if you are lucky. Throw a die once. Did you get a 6? Throw the die 3 times. How many times did you throw a 6? Draw a bar chart like this. Colour in a square for each number you throw.

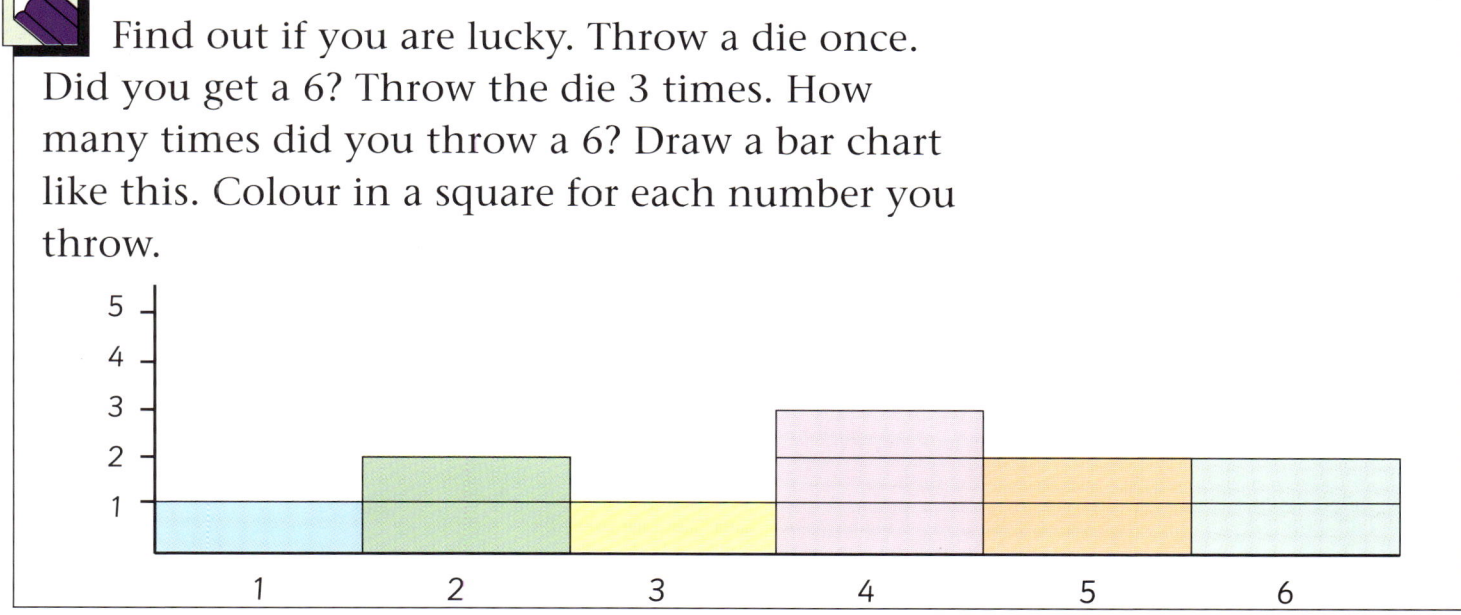

Rollercoaster game

You will need:

1 die

1 counter for each player

How to play:

1. Place all the counters on the *Start* square.
2. Take turns to throw the die.
3. Move you counter the number of squares shown on the die. You must move in the direction of the arrows.
4. If you land on a numbered square you must throw one of the numbers written on that square before you move on.
5. The first person to land on the *Finish* square is the winner.

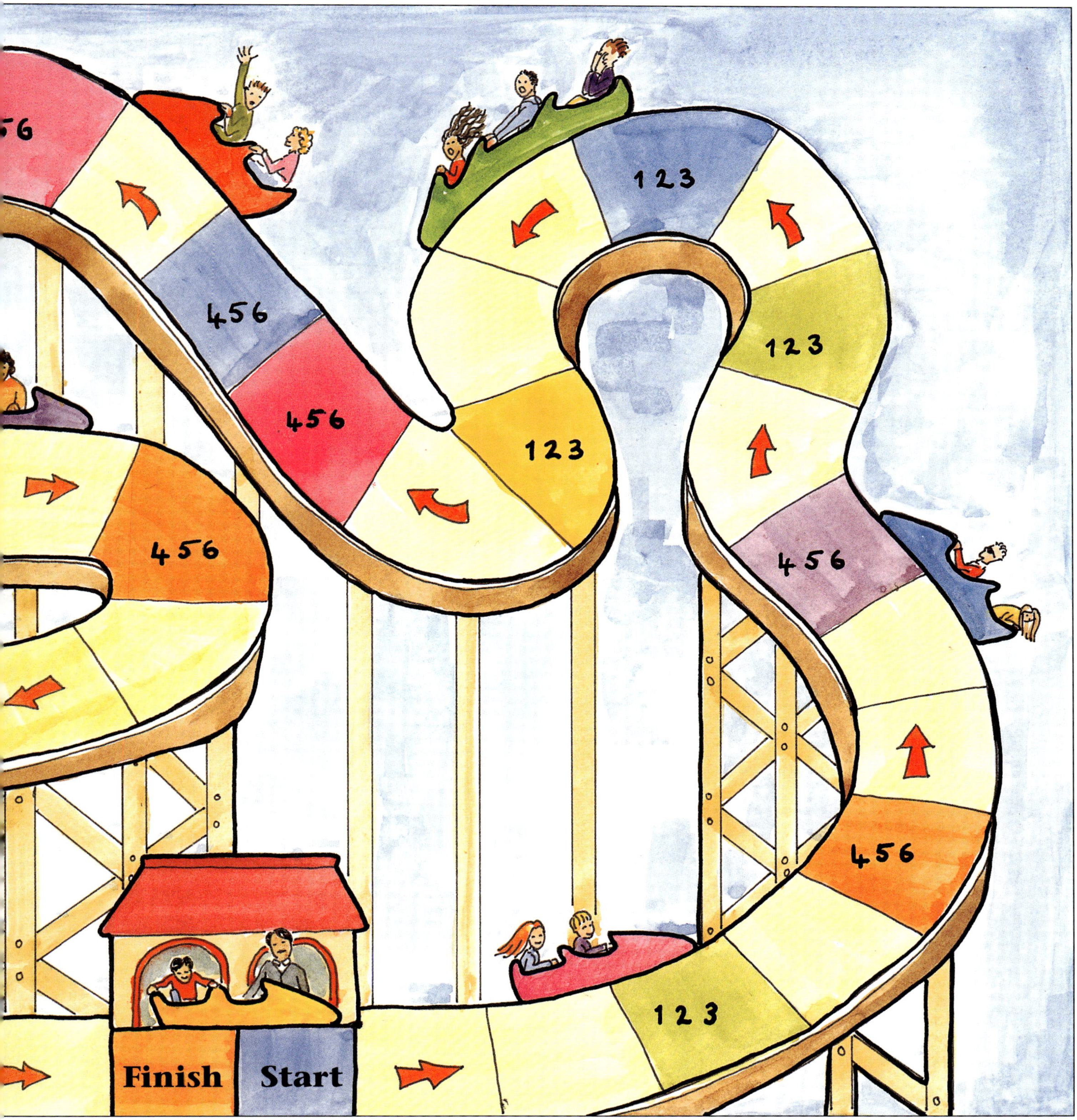

56
456
456
123
456
123
123
456
456
123
Finish
Start

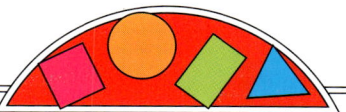

On the lake

Lakes are good places to go to see birds and animals. Sometimes you can go out in a boat on a lake.

Raoul and and his big sister Miranda have paid to take a rowing boat out for an hour. They paid with a £5.00 note. How much change did they get?

They decide to row to the islands. It takes 15 minutes to row there. How long will they have to play on the islands?

£3.50 for 1 hour

The islands are connected by bridges. Find a route for Raoul and Miranda to visit all the islands and get back to their boat. How many different routes can you find?

If the boat landed at another island would your answer be different?

At the zoo

Some animals live in zoos so that we can learn about them and look after them. The best time to see the animals is when they are eating.

Rajah eats 2 **kg** of meat at each meal. How much meat does he eat in a day? How much meat does he eat in a week? Sabu eats 3 kg at each meal. How much meat does he eat in a week? How much more meat does Sabu eat in one week than Rajah? Use counters or a calculator to help you find the answers.

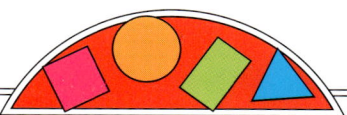

21

Jo is the zoo keeper. She wants to change the zoo so that no animal is beside one of its own kind. Can you help her do this?

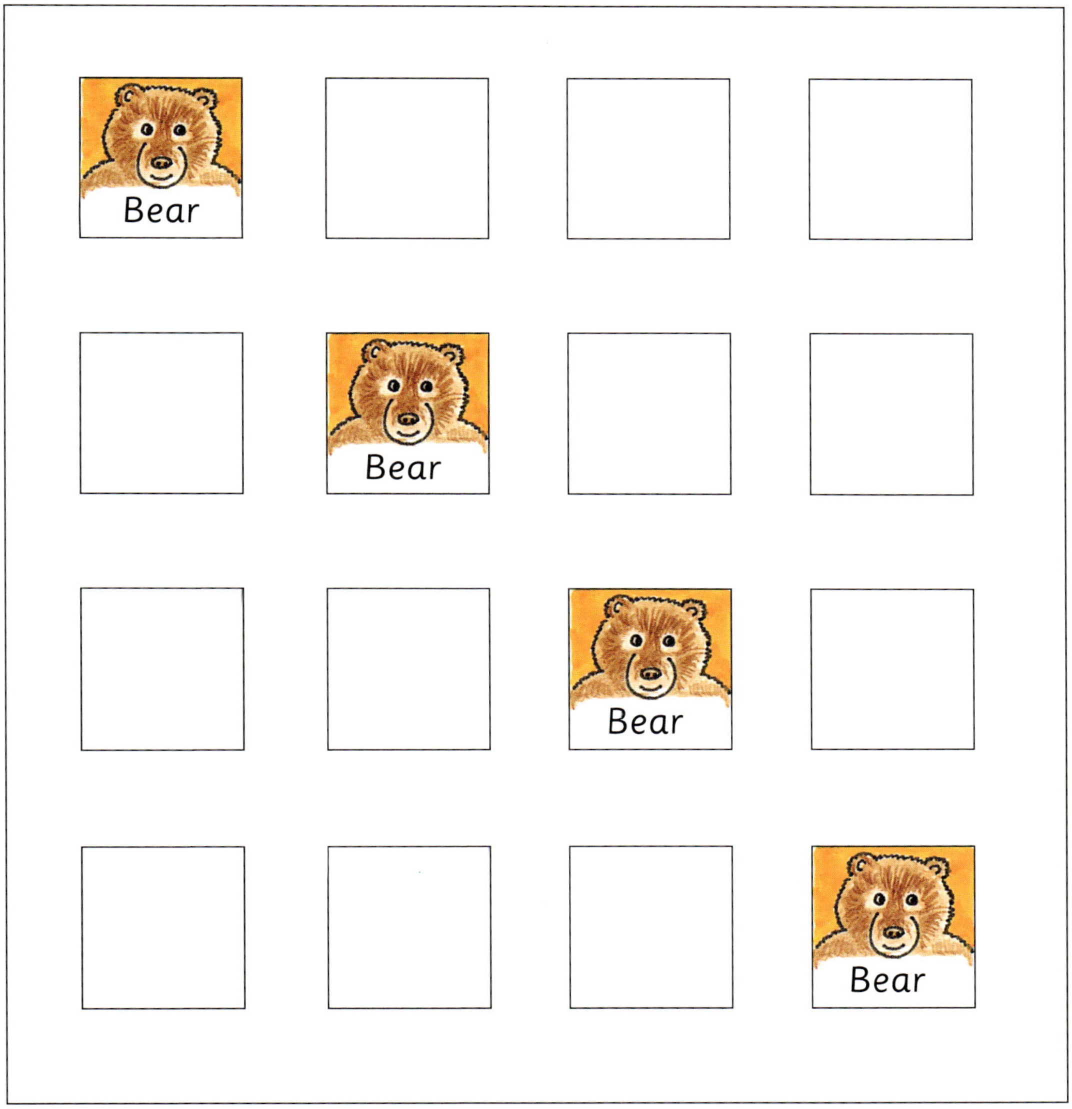

  Draw a chart like this.

Draw each animal on a small piece of paper. Put an animal in every space. Every row should have a lion, a monkey, a giraffe and a bear. Jo has put the bears on a **diagonal** line. Is this the best place for them?

Going for a swim

It is important to learn to swim. These children are at the swimming pool. Some people swim in the sea or in rivers and lakes. It is dangerous to swim in these places without an adult.

Pool Prices	
Adults	£1.00
Children	50p
Shampoo	20p
Goggle hire	25p
Cap hire	35p
Floats and wings	20p

Jill and Karen are going swimming with their aunt. How much will it cost for them all to get in? Jill wants to hire some goggles with her pocket money. She has 50p. How much change will she get?

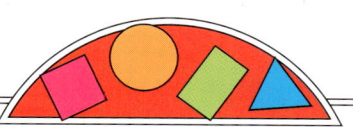

23

Ranjit takes 18 strokes to swim one length.
Mohammed can do a length in **half** as many strokes.
How many strokes does Mohammed take?

Write down this table and fill in all of the spaces. You can use counters to help you.

Ranjit	Mohammed
18	
20	
22	
24	
26	

A plane journey

Sonja is going on holiday to a country far away. She is going by plane.

Sonja is flying from Norway to Spain. The flight takes 3 hours. Can you guess which country she will be flying over after 1 hour? Where do you think she will be after 2 hours?

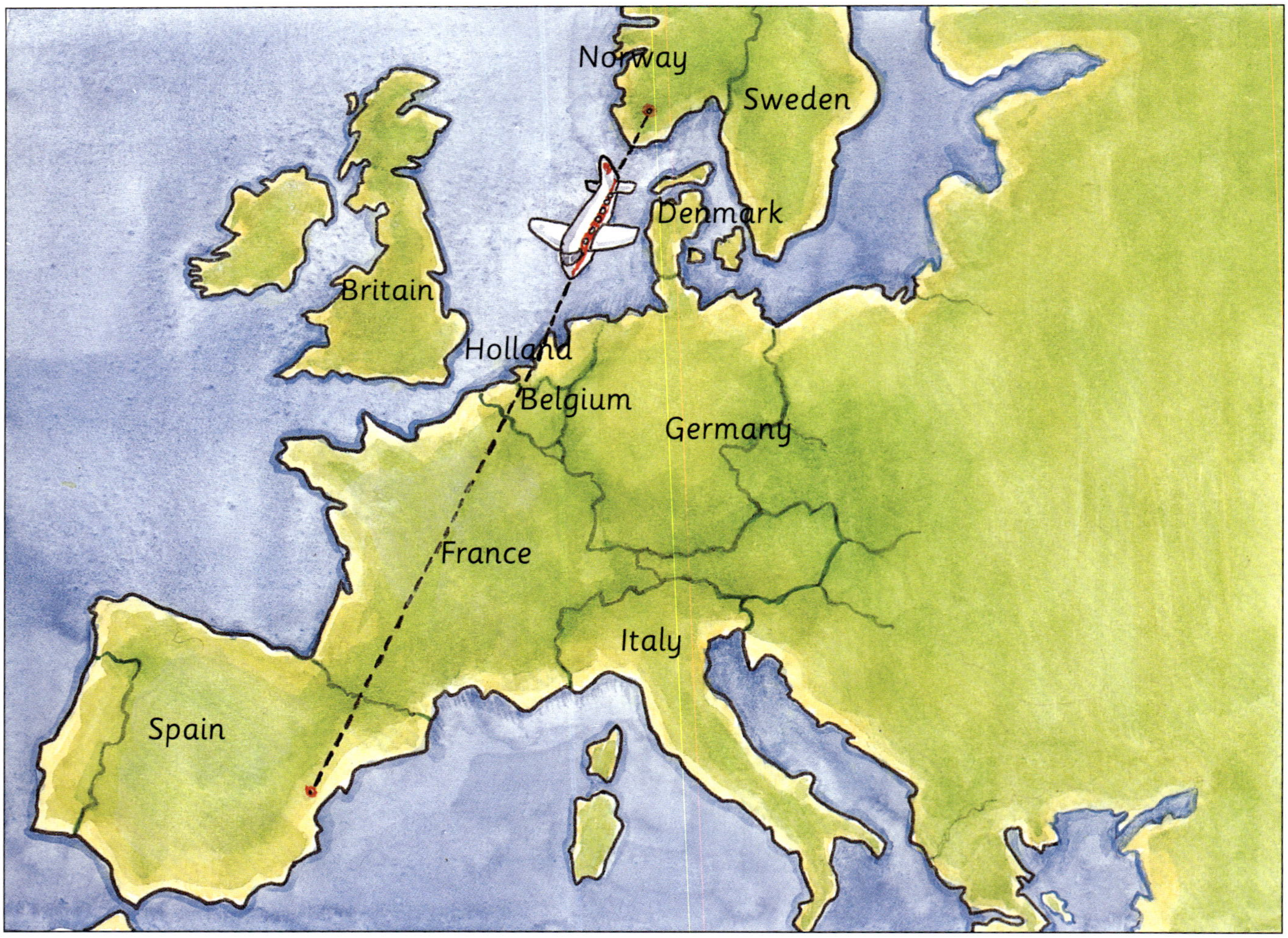

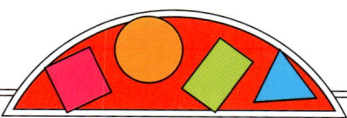

Half an hour after the plane takes off, the cabin staff give people lunch. The film starts an hour after take-off. Half an hour before the plane lands the cabin staff give people coffee and cakes.

Welcome to Norway Air

Take off	11.00 am
Lunch	
Film	12.00 noon
Coffee	
Landing	2.00 pm

We hope you enjoy your flight.

Draw your own timetable for Sonja's journey like this. Fill in the times that are missing.

Write out a timetable of your own for a flight that lasts 8 hours.

At the seaside

It is fun to go to the seaside. You can swim in the sea and play games on the beach. You can build lots of sandcastles on a sandy beach.

Tony makes a castle with a single bucket of sand. Paula builds a higher castle with three buckets of sand. Her older sister builds the next one with six buckets of sand.

On a piece of paper draw the next two sizes of sandcastle.

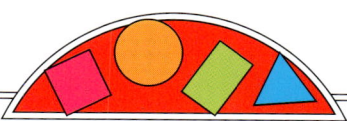

Paula wants to make different flags for each of the sandcastles. She only has squared paper and two different colours to use. If her flags have two squares, she can make four different flags.

Help Paula make flags with four squares. Each square can only have one colour in it.

Here are two.

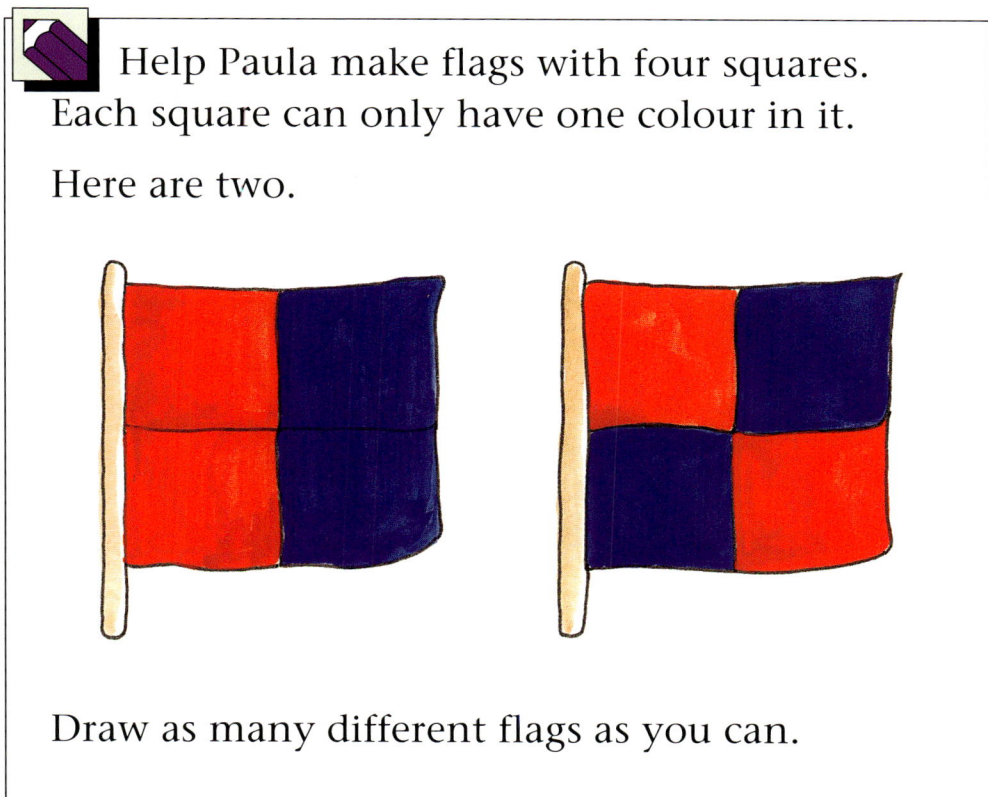

Draw as many different flags as you can.

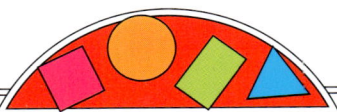

Glossary

Cylinder
A tube shape. The circles at the ends are the same size.

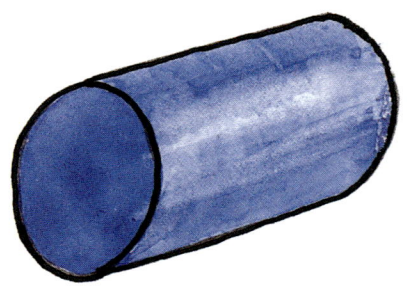

Cube
A solid shape with 6 faces. Each face is a square. A die is a cube.

Diagonal
A diagonal is a straight line joining two corners of a shape.

Directions
These describe the ways in which you move to get from one place to another. You need to use words like 'turn', 'left', 'right' and 'forward', when you give directions.

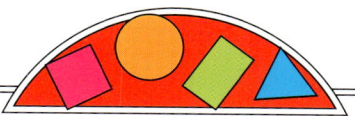

29

Half
A half is written like this: ½. It tells you the object or number has been divided into two equal parts.

kg
This is a short way of writing 'kilogram'. A kilogram is one of the units we use to describe how heavy something is.

Octagon
A flat shape with 8 sides.

Pentagon
A flat shape with 5 sides.

Route
The way from one place to another, going along paths or roads.

Symmetrical
A shape is symmetrical if it can be folded into halves and the two halves make a mirror picture of each other.

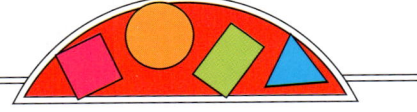

Notes for parents and teachers

Page 4/5

Symmetry can have several different meanings. This book deals only with reflectional or 'mirror' symmetry. The dotted line in the pictures represents the position of a mirror which would reflect the other half of the butterfly. A common error for young children is to draw patterns as though moved along rather than reflected. Children can be helped to understand this by holding a mirror on the dotted line and being asked to describe what they can see. The children could then draw the reflection bit by bit. This will encourage them to compare relative positions in the mirror image.

Page 6/7

A good activity for practising right and left. Marking a child's hands with R and L, using tape could help here. Young children can find map reading difficult and they may need to turn the map round to face the way the person is walking in order to follow or to give directions. Drawing a simplified map of the local area and then walking the actual routes with the children could help them to write down the directions more easily.

In the activity you can use string to determine which route is the longest.

Page 8/9

When talking about shapes with children, differentiate between flat (2D) shapes and solid (3D) shapes. Children can look for different shapes in the environment – inside and outside. Ask them to describe simple properties of shapes, such as the number of sides or, for solid shapes, the number of faces and corners and whether there are any square corners (right angles).

Page 10/11

Children often encounter digital time through the use of video recorders, digital watches etc. If this is the first time a child has seen time written in digital form, discuss the number of minutes in an hour and in a half hour, and the ways we write down time. The toy train puzzle is open ended to encourage children to think about number patterns and ways of solving the problem.

Page 12/13

These activities introduce simple multiplication and division. It will help the children to practise these simple operations if they repeat the activities using different objects. The supermarket activity could be extended by asking the children to draw their own layout for a supermarket and to discuss the best places for different foods. It will also reinforce the concept of direction.

Page 14/15

Young children often believe that a 'six' is more difficult to get, simply because it is often required to begin a game. Probability activities like this one should give a fairly even distribution of the numbers, so that children can see that 'six' is likely to be thrown as frequently as any other number on a die.

Page 16/17

Most children have played similar kinds of board games. Make sure they have counters for each player and dice, and that they understand the rules. Children could record the number of throws of the dice taken to win the game. This could be the target number of throws for the next game. It should be brought to childrens notice, as in the previous page, that the large numbers – 4, 5, 6 – are no harder to get than the small ones.

Page 18/19

There are a number of different answers to this puzzle. It is important that children have time to explore all the options. They should be able to describe the alternatives.

Page 20/21

The bears have been placed on a diagonal line to make the puzzle easier for children to solve. The other animals will also fall into place on diagonal lines. The exploration and discussion of the problems and solutions are the most important aspects of this activity. Children could then be asked to look for a solution which does not begin with the placing of any animal on a diagonal line.

Page 22/23

It is important to give children frequent opportunites to use and talk about money. The prices here have been chosen for ease of calculation. If the numbers are too large for a particular child to handle, model the prices with real or toy money. Discuss how many different ways they can make 50p with combinations of 20p, 10p and 5p pieces. If you wish to use a real price list, children may need to use calculators.

Page 24/25

This activity could be combined with any study of a different country or area. Travel agents can supply the flight times. It is best to ignore the time differences between countries, as most young children find this very difficult to understand. To follow up the estimation, a string marked with the hours can be stretched from the start to the finish of the journey on the map.

Page 26/27

The sandcastle puzzle produces triangle numbers – 1, 3, 6, 10, 15, 21 – so called because they can be arranged in a triangle shape. They are achieved by adding 1 more to the sum each time. Discuss the number pattern with the children and ask them what is added to the sum each time, and what is the difference between the numbers.

There are 16 different flags with 4 squares and 2 colours. This is too many for most children to find, but the search itself, and the ways in which they try to solve the problem is important.

A note about computers

If you have access to a simple database with graph facilities, then you can use any of the data collection activities in this book as an opportunity to introduce children to such software. Pie charts can then be used in place of barcharts in certain circumstances. Young children cannot draw pie charts, but they can recognize the relative sizes of the sections.

Index

B

bar chart   15

D

diagonals   21

directions   6, 7, 13

M

money   18, 22

P

patterns   5, 14, 26, 27

S

shapes   8, 9

symmetry   5

T

time   10, 18, 24, 25

timetable   10, 25

W

weighing   20